This edition published by
THE TASMANIAN BOOK COMPANY
34 St Andrews Circle
Launceston, Tasmania 7250

ISBN 1-875240-00-4

Copyright © 1993
The Tasmanian Book Company
Photographs Copyright ©
Dennis Harding
Typeset by
David Metcalfe

*PREVIOUS PAGE: The sun sets magnificently over the isthmus of Eaglehawk
Neck - leading to the Tasman Peninsula, and once guarded by fierce dogs as
the only escape route from the Port Arthur penal colony.*

Contents

The shadow of venerable conifers dapples Fitzpatrick's Inn, Westbury, a fine building in the dignified Georgian style which is typical of the early colonial period.

PREVIOUS PAGE: Great Oyster Bay. These waters offer one of the best in-shore fishing spots in Tasmania, abounding in top-class table fish including flathead, trumpeter and trevally.

T A S M A N I A

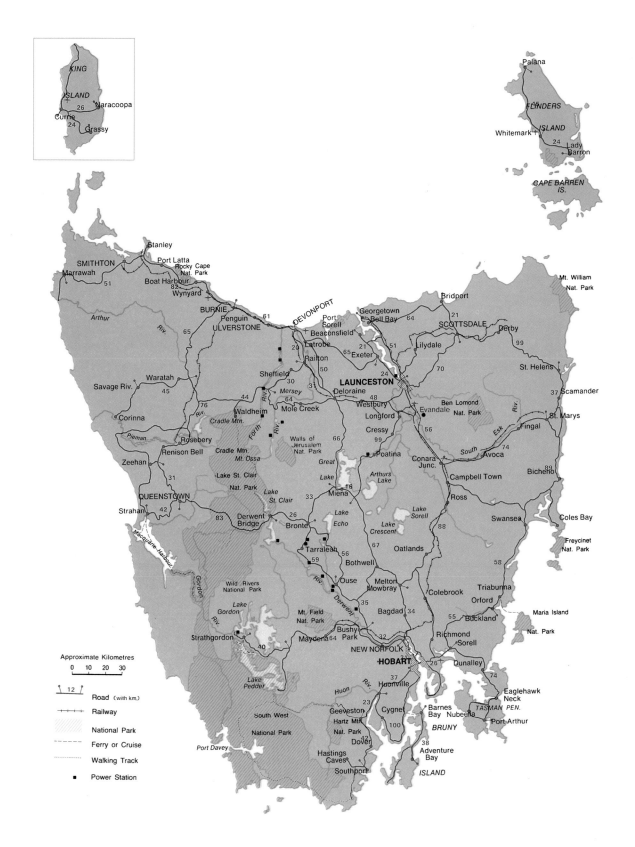

KING ISLAND
Currie 24 Grassy
26 Naracoopa

FLINDERS ISLAND
Palana
Whitemark 24 Lady Barron
CAPE BARREN IS.

Stanley
Port Latta
Rocky Cape Nat. Park
SMITHTON
Marrawah 51 Boat Harbour
82 Wynyard
BURNIE 61
Penguin ULVERSTONE 65
DEVONPORT
Port Sorell
Beaconsfield
Latrobe 21
65 Exeter
Railton 50
20
Sheffield 30 31
LAUNCESTON
Deloraine 48
24
Mersey 64
Westbury
Mole Creek
Longford
Cressy
Bridport
Georgetown Bell Bay 64
SCOTTSDALE 21
Lilydale
70 Derby 99
St. Helens
37 Scamander
Ben Lomond Nat. Park
Evandale 56
Esk Riv.
St. Marys
Fingal
South 74
Avoca
Bicheno 89
Campbell Town
Ross
Swansea
Coles Bay
Freycinet Nat. Park
58
Mt. William Nat. Park

Arthur Riv.
Savage Riv.
Waratah 45
76
Waldheim 44
Corinna
Cradle Mtn.
Pieman
Rosebery
Renison Bell
Zeehan
Forth Riv.
Cradle Mtn. Mt. Ossa
Lake St. Clair Nat. Park
Walls of Jerusalem Nat. Park 66
Great
Lake
Miena 16
Lake St. Clair
QUEENSTOWN 31
Strahan 42
83
Derwent Bridge 26
Bronte
33
Lake Echo
Arthurs Lake
99 Poatina
Conara Junc.
Lake Sorell
Lake Crescent 88
Oatlands
67
Tarraleah 59
56 Bothwell
Ouse
Melton Mowbray
35
Bagdad 34
Colebrook
Triabunna
Orford
Buckland 55
Maria Island Nat. Park

Macquarie Harbour
Gordon Riv.
Wild Rivers National Park
Lake Gordon
Lake Pedder
Mt. Field Nat. Park
Strathgordon
Maydena 64
Bushy Park
NEW NORFOLK
32
Derwent Riv.
HOBART
26 Dunalley 74
Richmond
Sorell
Eaglehawk Neck
TASMAN PEN.
Port Arthur

Huon Riv.
37 Huonville
23
Geeveston
Dover
42
Hastings Caves
Southport
Cygnet
Barnes Bay Nubeena
100
BRUNY
38 Adventure Bay
ISLAND

South West National Park
Port Davey

Approximate Kilometres
0 10 20 30

12 Road (with km.)
Railway
National Park
Ferry or Cruise
Walking Track
Power Station

9

Introduction

Lying in the path of the westerly wind belt known as the "Roaring Forties" is an island that bears a shape not unlike an ancient warrior's shield. The only other land masses which share this latitude are New Zealand and, to the west, many thousands of kilometres away, South America. The Earth's southern peoples occupy a decidedly oceanic hemisphere.

Australians from mainland States often express a jaundiced view of Tasmania's climatic regime, looking upon that small but rugged shield as providing a staunch defence (which is more than simply metaphorical) against any northward creep of the Antarctic ice. However, only when the salt-laden westerlies surrender occasionally to a fullblooded southerly do Tasmanians have any inkling of the presence of a major ice body anywhere in their part of the planet. In truth (except for the sub-Antarctic outlier of Macquarie Island), Tasmania has one of the healthiest and most equable climates in the world. To emphasize this point - if the Midland settlement of Campbell Town were transported to the northern hemisphere, it would sit on the same latitude as the northern suburbs of Rome.

Tasmania's land area, including that of its lesser islands, is 68,331 square kilometres, or 0.9 percent of the total area of Australia. Compared to the large island to the immediate north occupied by their political and cultural confreres, Tasmanians appear to possess a rather minuscule piece of real estate. Nevertheless, a glance at an atlas will reveal a number of sovereign countries which have a smaller area - Sri Lanka, Denmark and Switzerland among them.

Perhaps the most notable aspect of Tasmania's many attributes is its low population density. In contrast to the aforementioned countries, which measure their populations in millions, only 450,000 people live in Tasmania. In a State where most of the politicians seem inalienably married to the growth ethic, few of our leaders recognise our innate good fortune. However, to much of the world outside, already overburdened with human population, Tasmania must seem like a spacious wonderland.

Since the first British settlement was established at Risdon Cove, on the eastern bank of the Derwent River, in September 1803, the population has multiplied a hundredfold. Up until this time, the only human occupants were the Tasmanian Aborigines, black-skinned hunter-gatherers whose presence dates back at least 20,000 years. Descendants of those people still hold faith with the Aboriginal inheritance but, sadly, most of their original culture and much of their unique gene pool has been lost. It is the State's greatest tragedy.

Tasmania, however, is not a place where one dwells upon tragedies, for there is a great deal about this island that is good and much that is superlative. Out of the ashes of near-genocide and the grimness of its penal baptism, Tasmania has emerged as one of the world's fairest and most pleasant societies.

When the last convict vessel docked at Hobart Town on 26 May 1853, the first chapter in the colony's modern history began to draw to a close, and soon after that, its earlier name of "Van Diemen's Land" (bestowed by its Dutch discoverer Abel

Tasman in 1642) was changed to the present form. Three years later, responsible self-government was initiated with the setting up of a new bicameral parliament and, ever since, Tasmania has moved towards a steadily more democratic political structure. Tasmanian society is now resolutely wedded to the values of democracy, and its electoral system for the House of Assembly is considered by many commentators to be the fairest in the world.

Common decency is endemic in Tasmania. As free and unfettered citizens, the island's people have no suzerain masters, and class distinction is but a minor aspect of their social structure. Tasmanians, in general, have discarded hypertension from their list of social aspirations.

The unhurried pace of Tasmanian life, which is sometimes misinterpreted as evidence of a lack of sophistication, obscures the fact that here, as in much of the western world, traditional mores are being destroyed in the face of a concerted onslaught from the culture barons of New York, Los Angeles and London. However, if you look hard, you can still find an occasional country hall ringing to the cheerful tones of a bush dance or oldtime dance. When supper time is announced, ruddy large-boned men, buxom matrons, a horde of young children and a few teenagers brave enough to withstand the carpings of peers will devour the multifarious productions of a community which values its calories and has, as yet, neglected to be daunted by the notion that cholesterol is other than a gimmick organised by polyunsaturated-margarine companies. A bush dance is Tasmania *par excellence*. There should be more of them.

Despite these occasional welcome escapes from the world of whizz-bang electronics and flashing lights, Tasmanians utilise a technology as sophisticated as any. On the merest whim, and at a moment's notice, telephone receivers can be set jangling on the other side of the world. The world's latest gadgets are on display in factory, shop and home. This is no island swamped by quaint folksiness.

Nevertheless, the traveller will find much in Tasmania which is redolent of the world before the advent of nylon stockings and sliced bread, not to mention the nuclear bomb. A large number of stone buildings - constructed in the convict era - adorn our country towns, while split-paling bushman-built huts still dot parts of the central highlands and western mountains. Splendid homes of long-gone gentry emphasize that wealth, style and architectural grace were far from unknown during the early days of colonization.

Ultimately, however, it is the natural beauty with which Tasmania has been blessed that has the most lasting effect on the island's admirers. There are verdant rolling farmlands with soils so chocolate that you almost feel you could eat them, sheep with superfine wool that is the envy of the world, and the tallest hardwood forests on the planet. There are thousands of lakes, many stocked with hard-fighting trout, coastal cliffs and beaches which stand comparison with the best anywhere, unique and fascinating flora and fauna, and spreading vistas of untamed wilderness which serve as a spectacular reminder of how far we have come down the track of cultural evolution and, perhaps, how far we - as a species - have strayed from the footpath of wisdom in our dealings with the natural environment.

If ever there is a global award for natural splendour, Tasmania would surely be one of the most prominent candidates. One can only hope that, as the years pass, this magnificent heritage will be protected and that Tasmania will continue to be a place of pleasure and inspiration for residents and visitors alike.

SOUTH
&
SOUTH-EAST

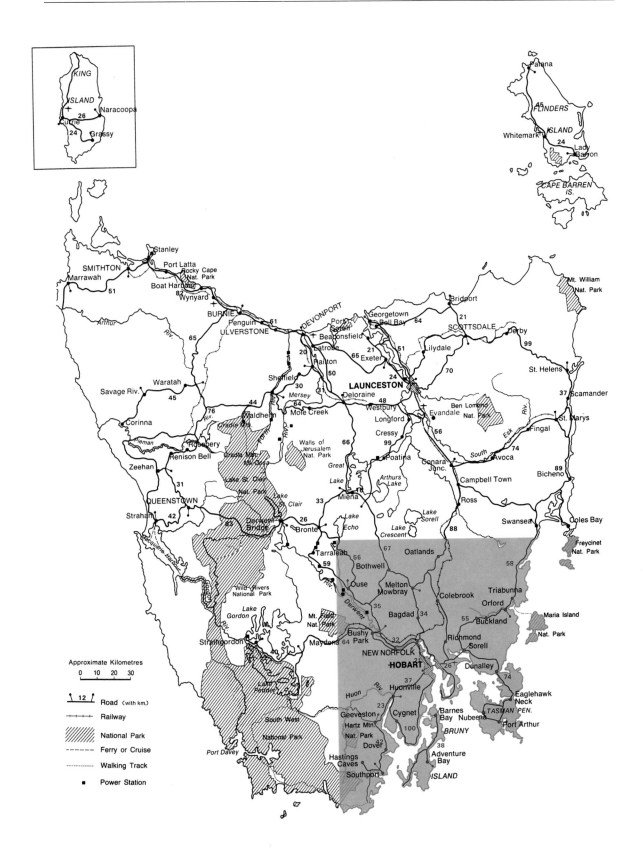

KING
ISLAND
26
Naracoopa
Currie
24
Grassy

Palana
FLINDERS
45
ISLAND
Whitemark
24
Lady Barron
CAPE BARREN
IS.

Stanley
SMITHTON
Port Latta
Rocky Cape
Nat. Park
Marrawah
Boat Harbour
51
82
Wynyard
BURNIE
Penguin
61
Mt. William
Nat. Park
Bridport
Georgetown
Bell Bay
64
21
SCOTTSDALE
Derby
ULVERSTONE
65
DEVONPORT
Port Sorell
Beaconsfield
Lilydale
99
Latrobe
21
51
Sheffield
20
Railton
65
Exeter
70
St. Helens
Savage Riv.
Waratah
30
50
LAUNCESTON
24
45
Mersey
Deloraine
37
Scamander
76
44
64
48
Riv.
Waldheim
Mole Creek
Westbury
Ben Lomond
Nat. Park
St. Marys
Corinna
Cradle Mtn.
Longford
Evandale
Fingal
Rosebery
Walls of
Jerusalem
Nat. Park
66
Cressy
56
74
Avoca
Renison Bell
Zeehan
Cradle Mtn.
Mt. Ossa
Great
99
Poatina
Bicheno
89
Lake St. Clair
Nat. Park
Lake
Conara
Junc.
Campbell Town
31
Lake
St. Clair
33
Miena
Arthurs
Lake
Ross
QUEENSTOWN
Lake
Echo
Lake
Crescent
Lake
Sorell
88
Swansea
Coles Bay
Strahan
42
Bronte
26
Derwent
Bridge
83
Freycinet
Nat. Park
Tarraleah
67
Oatlands
58
56
Bothwell
59
Ouse
Melton
Mowbray
Colebrook
Triabunna
Wild Rivers
National Park
35
Bagdad
34
Orford
Lake
Gordon
Mt. Field
Nat. Park
Bushy
Park
32
55
Buckland
Maria Island
Nat. Park
Maydena
64
Richmond
Sorell
NEW NORFOLK
21
Strathgordon
40
HOBART
26
Dunalley
37
74
Huon
Huonville
Eaglehawk
Neck
Lake
Pedder
23
Cygnet
Barnes
Bay
Nubeena
TASMAN PEN.
Geeveston
Port Arthur
South West
National Park
Hartz Mtn.
Nat. Park
100
BRUNY
Dover
38
Adventure
Bay
Port Davey
Hastings
Caves
Southport
ISLAND

Approximate Kilometres

0 10 20 30

12 Road (with km)

++++ Railway

///// National Park

- - - - Ferry or Cruise

.... Walking Track

■ Power Station

13

In September 1803, Lieutenant John Bowen took his pioneering party ashore at Risdon Cove on the eastern bank of the Derwent River. Some months later, the British government decided to establish a settlement at Port Phillip (near modern Melbourne) and dispatched the former deputy judge-advocate of New South Wales, David Collins, to this end. Collins, however, found Port Phillip to be unsuitable and he took the significant decision to move his expedition south to the Derwent. Latter-day Tasmanians would simply regard this as an example of his innate good taste!

Collins was unimpressed, however, by Risdon Cove and he moved the entire settlement to Sullivan's Cove on the western bank of the river to make use of a deeper anchorage and a better water supply. The city of Hobart was born.

It is easy to imagine that Collins was a man motivated by a sense of aesthetic destiny, for he gave to Tasmania's capital one of the most splendid settings of any city in the world. Watching over the scene is the moody bulk of Mount Wellington, rearing to an altitude of 1,270 metres, a ready reminder of the rugged and dissected nature of Tasmania's topography. Below, spreading out to the south, is the Derwent estuary, which, in bygone days, was the island's maritime gateway. For many expeditions, it was (and remains) the last sight of settled lands before encountering the frozen wastes of the Antarctic.

Hobart is today a modern bustling city, armed with large heavy industries, which has its own diminutive version of daily rush-hour madness, but its saving grace is its proximity to the natural environment which is Tasmania's recurring theme. When you look around, you can always see eucalypt-clad hillsides or the dolerite spires of "The Mountain". Many people still go out to nearby country areas, armed with a chainsaw and trailer, to obtain a winter's wood supply and, in summertime, unspoiled beaches are little more than a long stone's-throw away.

For the traveller who wishes to taste the atmosphere of old Hobart Town, a walk from historic Salamanca Place into the quiet, narrow streets of Battery Point is highly recommended. The other "must" is a journey to the stark summit of Mount Wellington (but take some warm clothes). For the adventurous, a Hobart company even runs bicycle trips down to the city from the summit - freewheeling all the way!

In 1830, a penal station was set up on the Tasman Peninsula, in the far South-East. The peninsula is a beautiful place where the olive tones of eucalypt forest blend with the greens of farmland and the blue of the sea. However, one little doubts that the convicts who were incarcerated there had a less favourable outlook on their abode than we do today. The ruins of the buildings which were built and used during the forty-seven years of Port Arthur's occupancy as a penal settlement are some of the finest architectural relics of Australia's early colonial period. Indeed, Port Arthur has been for many years the State's premier tourist attraction.

The coastline of the Tasman Peninsula is one of Tasmania's finest. It boasts spectacular dolerite cliffs and the windswept starkness of Tasman Island as well as delightful sandy beaches and gentle, wooded shorelines. There can be few better places to engage in the exciting sport of tuna fishing. Even when the fish are not biting, the wild coastal scenery ensures an enjoyable day out. Inevitably, of course, the heaving swell of the Tasman Sea dictates that a decided strength of stomach is a characteristic which contributes to the pleasure of the experience!

Also of particular note in the southern part of the East Coast is Maria Island National Park. The island once resounded to the labours of convicts, farmers and a large cement-manufacturing industry, but it is now a place of peace except, perhaps, for the occasional troubled ghost of a long-dead convict which flits among the old ruins. It is a wonderful place for the student of Tasmanian history and for those interested in fossils, for the limestone cliffs near Darlington are packed full of petrified examples of long-extinct marine life.

Closer to Hobart is Richmond, another unspoiled and historic little town which acts as an advertisement for all that is good about sandstone. The town's best-known feature is Australia's oldest bridge, completed in 1825. There are other places, too, like Buckland and Swansea, where old buildings remain to intrigue the modern citizen, and numerous settlements on or close to the Midland Highway which originally sat adjacent to the nineteenth-century coaching road between Hobart and Launceston. The Midland Highway, despite being the State's most important road, passes through largely unspoiled pastoral landscapes and retains, even in the late twentieth century, much of the atmosphere of the early colonial period. Towns like Oatlands, when viewed from afar, still possess the pleasant solidity bestowed by Tasmanian sandstone.

One of the best-loved collections of old buildings belongs to the property known as Lovely Banks built by grazier John Bisdee, who fell in love with the area after rounding up stray cattle there in 1820. Amid the rolling hills is an arrangement of stone buildings which, in their rustic simplicity, seem to have been placed there simply to please the eye. Mind you, life was once not so easy, for this was the country of the Van Diemen's Land bushrangers, desperadoes who challenged the authority of the Crown and who would descend, from time to time, to relieve the gentlefolk of the Midlands of their burden of excess wealth.

The highway between the State's two major population centres - for locals and visitors alike - was for long the predominant locality where people could interact with the native bush. Unfortunately, this granted Tasmania a burdensome legacy, for the Midlands - dry, slightly elevated, largely free of dense forest or scrub and remote from mountain country - are atypical. Certainly this region, in places, bears minor similarities to England in the solid homes, green (but only in winter and spring) paddocks, planted hedgerows and European trees, but to have referred to Tasmania as a "little England down under" was to have ignored the vast majority of the island - rugged, dramatic, forested, remote from civilization - which bore no resemblance to England whatsoever. Tasmania shall yet have its day. While earlier judges of the "Antipodes" chose to emphasize the similarities with their "civilized" homelands, new generations will come to view wildness and uniqueness as by far the more important attributes of this fortunate part of the world.

South of Hobart lie the Channel and Huon districts. D'Entrecasteaux Channel - surely one of Australia's loveliest waterways - divides mainland Tasmania from the elongate Bruny Island. Along its wooded shores are numerous settlements, large and small, some of which are effectively dormitory suburbs of Hobart, others of which are self-contained and somewhat isolated communities. Bruny Island itself is Tasmania in microcosm, ranging from the dry eucalypt-wooded north to the damp hilly forests of the south.

The Huon, around the lower reaches of the Huon River, was one of the world's greatest apple-growing areas, and it still retains some of its orchards, but only as relics of what was once considered a fail-safe industry. The first apple exports to Britain took place in 1891. While agriculture has diversified, the region's important forest industries have lost much of their earlier colour and variety. The small family-owned sawmills, once so characteristic of the Tasmanian bush, have slowly given way to large-scale clear-felling forestry based upon integration of saw-log retrieval with the controversial woodchip industry. One can only hope that forestry will be managed with extreme sensitivity, for the Huon is one of the most beautiful settled areas in the whole country. Only a short distance to the west is the South-West wilderness which carries a different beauty altogether.

Another gateway to the South-West is the Derwent Valley, which includes the historic settlement of New Norfolk, many farms and some hop plantations. A little to the west, diverging from the route of the Derwent, are the highlands of Mount Field National Park, drawing bushwalkers, sightseers and skiers. This region is dramatic for its sudden east-west transition from a country of dry, open rolling hills to the wet and craggy western mountains.

Maria Island, seen from the mouth of the Prosser River, Orford. The island is a beautiful place which boasts abundant wildlife and a fascinating history. It has been a national park since 1972 and is readily accessible thanks to a regular boat service from Louisville, north of Orford.

View over the misty South-West from the Hartz Mountains National Park. The high country of this park is accessible by road from the town of Geeveston, south of Huonville.

A summer sunrise from the observation platform on the summit of Mt Wellington (1,270 metres) near Hobart.

Spanning the Coal River is the Richmond Bridge, Australia's oldest. Commenced in December 1823 and completed in January 1825, it was built by convict labour to the design of Major Bell of the 48th Regiment. It is situated at the eastern end of the historic town of Richmond.

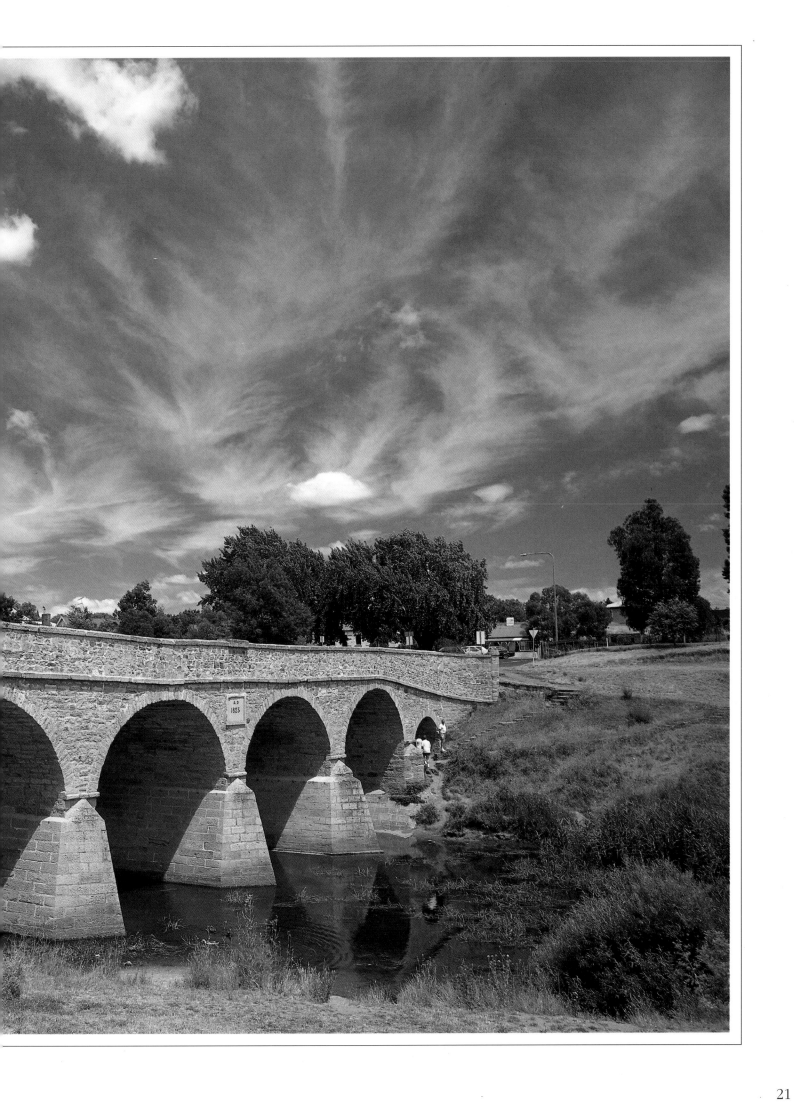

Snow-capped Mt Wellington and the city of Hobart, as seen across the Derwent River from the Bluff Reserve at Bellerive.

Cascade Brewery. Nestled in a valley between Hobart city and the dark bulk of Mt Wellington, this enterprise is the oldest functioning brewery in Australia. Its site was originally occupied by a women's penitentiary.

Hobart at dusk, seen from the hill above Sandy Bay.
At left is the Wrest Point Casino.

Wrest Point Casino and the Convention Centre, Sandy Bay, Hobart.

Elizabeth Street Mall, Hobart.

Charming cottages line Arthur's Circus in Battery Point, Hobart. Although situated close to the centre of the State's capital city, much of Battery Point has retained a pleasing historic ambience. It is a place of quiet streets and friendly cats, more suited to foot traffic than to motor vehicles.

LEFT: Historic Salamanca Place, Hobart. Old waterside warehouses are now occupied by galleries, shops, restaurants and community centres. The paved street is the site of the weekend open-air Salamanca Market, much frequented by locals and visitors alike.

RIGHT: The Cat and Fiddle Arcade provides traffic-free access to a large number of shops between Elizabeth and Murray Streets, Hobart.

The Tasman Bridge at night from Rosny Hill on Hobart's eastern shore. The bridge was opened in 1964, but on 5 January 1975 the Lake Illawarra, an ore-carrying ship bound upriver, collided with it and broke it in two, causing the deaths of twelve people. This vital link between Hobart's eastern and western shores was re-opened on 8 October 1977.

Looking east from the summit of Mt Wellington towards Hobart and the Derwent River. The Tasman Bridge is visible at centre left.

LEFT: The shot tower, Taroona. Built single-handedly by Joseph Moir in 1870, this stone structure stands at the edge of the Channel Highway, south of Hobart. At the top of the 197-foot-high structure, molten lead was poured through a colander. As the molten droplets fell through the air and into water at the base, they solidified into spherical pellets. The tower ceased to be used for shot-making in 1904.

BELOW: Occupying an old stage-coach inn south of Hobart at Taroona is Tudor Court, where many of the visitors are welcomed by Hobart's town crier, Vic Garth. Inside is the Tudor Model Village, based on the English village of Chilham, which was constructed by John Palotta (1922-1971). Palotta was crippled by polio at nine years of age, and spent the rest of his days in a wheelchair. Able to use only one hand, he took twelve years to build the scale-model village.

Mecca for yachtsmen, and finishing point for the annual classic blue-water Sydney-to-Hobart race, Tasmania's capital has always had a strong maritime connections. This marina, watched over by the distinctive tower of the Wrest Point Casino, is situated between Battery Point and Sandy Bay.

The Japanese Garden, Botanical Gardens, Hobart. Situated on the eastern side of the Queen's Domain, facing the Derwent River, and adjacent to Government House, the Botanical Gardens are a much-loved feature of Tasmania's largest city.

Water sports on the Huon River at Huonville, south-west of Hobart.

The Plenty Salmon Ponds, Derwent Valley. Situated thirteen kilometres upriver from New Norfolk, the salmon ponds are run as a hatchery by the Inland Fisheries Commission. The first successful shipment of trout ova from Britain to Plenty took place in 1864 and, since that time, Tasmania has developed a reputation as one of the world's finest trout fisheries. The hatchery is open to the general public.

A pastoral scene at Port Arthur, Tasman Peninsula. In the distance is the church, on which work started in 1834. Only the shell remains, the roof and thirty-metre-high steeple having been destroyed by fire.

PREVIOUS PAGE: Sunrise on the Tessellated Pavement, Eaglehawke Neck. This natural feature, which is to be found close to the isthmus that connects the Forestier and Tasman Peninsulas, provides a classic example of cross-jointing in an ancient bed of mudstone.

The old penitentiary, Port Arthur. The former convict settlement is Tasmania's premier tourist attraction, enticing nearly half of the State's visitors. Established in 1830, it played host to 12,500 convicts before its closure in 1877.

Ruined buildings, Port Arthur. In the background is the four-storey brick penitentiary, the largest building in the former penal settlement. Originally designed as a store and granary, it held a maximum of 657 convicts.

The rugged coastline of the Tasman Peninsula near Cape Hauy.

Dramatic dolerite cliffs meet the Tasman Sea near Cape Pillar, Tasman Peninsula.

Sarah Kate, the charming little engine which regularly "steams up" on the narrow-gauge railway at the Bush Mill, Port Arthur.

KING
ISLAND
26
Naracoopa
Currie
24
Grassy

Palana
FLINDERS 45
ISLAND
Whitemark
24
Lady
Barron
CAPE BARREN
IS.

Stanley
Port Latta
Rocky Cape
Nat. Park
SMITHTON
Marrawah
Boat Harbour
51
Wynyard
82
BURNIE
Penguin
61
DEVONPORT
Port
Sorell
Georgetown
Bell Bay
64
Bridport
Mt. William
Nat. Park
ULVERSTONE
65
Beaconsfield
Latrobe
21
51
SCOTTSDALE
Derby
Arthur
Riv.
20
Railton
65
Exeter
Lilydale
99
50
St. Helens
Sheffield
Deloraine
LAUNCESTON
70
24
Waratah
30
31
Mersey
Westbury
48
Scamander
Savage Riv.
45
64
Mole Creek
Longford
Evandale
Ben Lomond
Nat. Park
37
St. Marys
44
Waldheim
Cressy
56
Esk
Riv.
Fingal
Corinna
76
Cradle Mtn.
North
66
99
74
Tieman
Riv.
Walls of
Jerusalem
Nat. Park
Poatina
Conara
Junc.
South
Avoca
Rosebery
Cradle Mtn.
Mt. Ossa
Arthurs
Lake
Campbell Town
89
Bicheno
Zeehan
Renison Bell
Lake St. Clair
Nat. Park
Great
Lake
Ross
31
Lake
St. Clair
33
Miena
16
Coles Bay
QUEENSTOWN
42
Lake
Echo
Lake
Sorell
Swansea
Strahan
83
Derwent
Bridge
26
Bronte
Lake
Crescent
88
Freycinet
Nat. Park
Tarraleah
67
Oatlands
58
Macquarie Harbour
59
56
Bothwell
Wild Rivers
National Park
Ouse
Melton
Mowbray
Colebrook
Triabunna
Lake
Gordon
35
Orford
Maria Island
Nat. Park
Mt. Field
Nat. Park
Bagdad
34
55
Buckland
Strathgordon
40
Bushy
Park
Maydena 64
NEW NORFOLK
32
Richmond
Sorell
Lake
Pedder
26
Dunalley
74
HOBART
37
Huon
Riv.
Huonville
Eaglehawk
Neck
South West
National Park
23
Geeveston
Cygnet
Barnes
Bay
Nubeena
TASMAN PEN.
Port Arthur
Hartz Mtn.
Nat. Park
100
BRUNY
Port Davey
Dover
42
38
Adventure
Bay
Hastings
Caves
Southport
ISLAND

Approximate Kilometres
0 10 20 30

12   Road (with km.)
     Railway
     National Park
     Ferry or Cruise
     Walking Track
■   Power Station

While David Collins was still at Port Phillip, considering his future movements, he sent his namesake William Collins to take a look at Port Dalrymple, in the Tamar estuary, on the north coast of Tasmania. By the time the junior Collins returned (with a favourable report), his superior had determined upon the move to the Derwent but, within a short time, Governor King of the parent colony, New South Wales, decided to establish another colony at Port Dalrymple. The leader of the pioneering expedition was Lieutenant-Colonel William Paterson, who arrived at the site of George Town on 4 November 1804 with 181 soldiers and convicts in four ships. He established York Town (near Beauty Point) as his headquarters, but this was deemed unsuitable and in March 1806 the settlement was moved to near the confluence of the South Esk and North Esk Rivers - the present site of Launceston.

In 1812, the northern colony was made subordinate to Hobart, but those few years of independence ensured that northern Tasmanians would never fully respect the right of southerners to control the seat of government, particularly as Launceston grew in wealth and influence. Thus does Governor King's legacy impinge upon the unity of modern Tasmanians. The rivalry continues today, and it is more than just playful parochialism. In mainland States, the capital city dwarfs all contenders for the title of largest population centre but, in Tasmania, Launceston has never been so far behind Hobart, in terms of size or influence.

Launceston is today a city of modest proportions, containing some 70,000 souls. In the last two decades it has improved its character, promoting the elegant and renovating the seedy, and it boasts many fine buildings and a number of beautiful parks. Some of its suburbs possess a characterless, power-line-bestrewn sprawl but, as always, just beyond the city's never-distant perimeter are the green fields, the olive eucalypt forests and the blue of mountains.

In the afternoon of Sunday 8 December 1811, the Governor of New South Wales, Lachlan Macquarie, entered the embryonic township of Launceston with his entourage. He was deeply impressed by what he saw:

" The grand view and noble picturesque landscape that presented themselves on our first coming in sight of Launceston and the three rivers, and fertile plains and lofty mountains by which they are bounded, were highly gratifying and truly sublime, and equal in point of beauty to anything I have ever seen in any country."

Macquarie bore witness to the extravagant beauty of an island which had been as yet little changed by Europeans. Even now, however, the vistas from Launceston, particularly towards the east, are largely those of native Tasmania. The Ben Lomond massif, one of the island's most elevated mountain plateaux, hangs as a distant backdrop to the city. It is at its best in deep winter when, caked with snow, it sits under a cloudless sky, beckoning the skier. It is Tasmania's premier ski resort but the skiing season is extremely short. A mild maritime climate has preserved our mountains from the worst ravages of ski-field development, while still allowing the genuine enthusiast access to his or her favoured sport for about three months of the year.

To the north of Ben Lomond are Mounts Barrow and Arthur, each in turn diminishing in stature. Mount Arthur stands above the township of Lilydale, in an area of rolling hills and green farms where, on a bright winter's morning, the interplay of frost, mist and sunshine makes a delightful scene. Near here are three popular tourist attractions: Bridestowe Lavender Farm, the W.A.G. Walker Rhododendron Reserve at Lalla and the Hollybank Forest Reserve at Underwood.

The Tamar River flows north-west from Launceston to meet the sea near George Town. It meanders through beautiful country, and there are many pleasant settlements along its banks. Like the Huon, it was also a great contributor to Tasmania's reputation as the "Apple Isle". One of the major tributaries of the Tamar is the South Esk, which has cut a spectacular passage through the Cataract Gorge, close to the centre of Launceston. The First Basin in the gorge is a popular recreational locale.

Upstream from this is the old Duck Reach power station which made Launceston a pioneer of hydro-electricity in 1895. In later decades, the South Esk was dammed to form Trevallyn Lake, from which the water was diverted to the Trevallyn Power Station. The thundering floods which devastated part of Launceston in 1929 can no longer occur because the water volume coming down the gorge is now controlled by the Hydro-Electric Commission. However, after prolonged heavy rain, the excess water in Trevallyn Lake pours over the spillway, recreating scenes of turbulent riverine fury which were once all too familiar to Launcestonians.

The South Esk has a gigantic catchment, for it describes an enormous semi-circular sweep from its origin in the hills close to the East Coast. It flows west along the wide Fingal Valley, spread along which are the old towns of Fingal and Avoca, before turning north and passing through the equally historic towns of Evandale and Perth. Beyond Fingal, to the east, is the mild East Coast, popular with holidaymakers for its pleasant climate and sandy beaches. It also has a sizeable fishing industry, and boats can be readily viewed in such ports as St Helens and Bicheno. South of Bicheno is one of the State's oldest and most popular national parks. Occupying virtually the entire Freycinet Peninsula and adjacent Schouten Island, Freycinet National Park - proclaimed in 1916 - is renowned for its attractive beaches. Winter is the best season to visit this lovely place, unique on the East Coast for its rugged granitic topography - when the creeks are running and the sea sparkles.

At the northernmost tip of the East Coast is Mount William National Park, where "Mountain" is a classic case of exaggeration (it reaches a staggering 218 metres above sea level!). This is fine, gentle coastal country where special consideration is given to the conservation of the native forester kangaroo. Sweeping west of this, along the North Coast, are beef-cattle country, swathes of sand dunes and, inland, well-watered dairy and arable farming lands, and hills which harbour significant patches of rainforest.

West and south-west of Launceston are fertile farmlands and further old towns, with the beauty of the Western Tiers always visible to the south. The Tiers are a dramatic escarpment on top of which lies the Central Plateau. This highland region is the angler's favoured location, for there are many lakes which invite exploration and numerous large trout awaiting capture. On the slopes of the Tiers are forests and numerous creeks and waterfalls which delight the visitor and provide a ready temptation to the avid photographer.

South of Launceston, on the route to Hobart, are the Midlands, renowned for their superfine wool production and for historic architectural relics. Arguably the most attractive town is Ross, where the old convict-built sandstone bridge stands close to some other fine old stone buildings. Viewed from the Midland Highway on a summer's evening, the spires, chimneys and solid silhouettes of Ross look very much as if they have stepped out of a history book.

In Bass Strait, off the north-eastern tip of the Tasmanian mainland, is the Furneaux Group of islands. The largest is Flinders Island, an attractive and windy place where the vistas are dominated by the sea and the rugged jumble of the Strzelecki Range in the island's south-west. Immediately to its south is Cape Barren Island, a wild and virtually roadless place which is well-known as a refuge of the Tasmanian Aborigines. Families of mixed Aboriginal and European heritage settled there in the nineteenth century.

Entally House, Hadspen. Built by Thomas Reibey in 1820, this historic abode is now owned by the Tasmanian Government and is run by the National Trust. It is set up as an example of a wealthy settler's estate of the early nineteenth century, and is open to the public.

Sunrise on the Tamar River at Deviot.

A tranquil morning scene on the Tamar River at Deviot.

ABOVE: Penny Royal Village, Launceston. This attractive tourist drawcard occupies an old quarry site adjacent to the mouth of the Cataract Gorge.

LEFT: Visitors enjoy the nautical attractions at Penny Royal World, Launceston. A canal, plied by various vessels, runs around the whole Penny Royal Gunpowder Mill complex.

The *Lady Stelfox* paddle steamer negotiates the waters of the Cataract Gorge, Launceston. Built on the banks of the Tamar River, the vessel has a shallow-draughted design based upon that of steamers on North America's Yukon River.

King's Bridge and the Cataract Gorge, Launceston. Prefabricated in England, the bridge - which connects Launceston city to the hillside suburb of Trevallyn - was floated into position in December 1863.

Autumn embraces the wooded hillsides of the Cataract Gorge, Launceston.

*The fountain, Prince's Square, Launceston. The native scrub was first cleared here in 1824
and the fountain installed in 1859. It was cast in iron - and then surface-bronzed - as a copy
of an original in Paris designed by M. Lienard, an eminent French sculptor. The square,
now one of the city's loveliest parks, was named for the Duke of Edinburgh in 1868.*

*Shoppers enjoy the relaxed atmosphere
of the Quadrant Mall, Launceston.*

The leafy tranquillity of City Park, Launceston. The building at left is the John Hart Conservatory, famed for its colourful display of flowers. Other attractions of the park are its monkey island and duck pond.

Completed in 1838 for James Cox, Clarendon is situated in the northern Midlands some twenty kilometres south-east of Launceston. It is one of Tasmania's grandest houses, and has been owned by the National Trust since 1962.

ABOVE: The historic village Evandale, south of Launceston. Lachlan Macquarie, Governor of New South Wales, camped here in 1811, calling the place "Honeysuckle Bank". The present name (originally "Evansdale") was given in honour of George William Evans, Surveyor-General of Van Diemen's Land.

LEFT: The small town of Longford, south of Launceston, retains much of its historic charm. This area was first settled by Europeans in 1808 and given the name of Norfolk Plains since many of the settlers came from Norfolk Island. The township was surveyed in 1814 and called Latour. The name was changed to Longford in 1833.

Franklin House, on the southern outskirts of Launceston. Built by Britton Jones in 1838, it was for a time a boy's school noted for its severe discipline. The National Trust bought it and restored it in 1960, furnishing it in Georgian style. It is open to the public.

A touch of Switzerland in rural Tasmania. Situated some fifteen kilometres from Launceston, the village of Grindelwald possesses an old-world charm inspired by its Swiss namesake. In the background is the lakeside church.

Batman Bridge and the Tamar River. Named after John Batman, an early citizen of Van Diemen's Land who helped to found the city of Melbourne, this attractive structure was opened on 18 May 1968.

Early mining technology is displayed in the gold-mine museum at Beaconsfield, West Tamar.

The Bridestowe Lavender Farm, Golconda, north-east of Launceston, has grown markedly since C.K. Denny established a fifth of a hectare of lavender plants in 1924. January is the best month to see this enterprise, when the countless rows of flowers are being harvested for their oil. It is open to the public only during the harvesting season.

Aerial view of Wineglass Bay, Freycinet Peninsula, East Coast. Situated close to the holiday township of Coles Bay, the peninsula has been a national park since August 1916.

This view along Wineglass Bay, on the Freycinet Peninsula, displays the rugged peacefulness and uncrowded landscape of Tasmania's East Coast - a favourite holiday destination.

Coastline near Boulder Point, Mt William National Park.

Aerial view along the Bay of Fires to the popular holiday settlement of Binalong Bay, East Coast.

Meetus Falls lie forty kilometres from Swansea, off the Lake Leake Road to Campbell Town. Access is at weekends only, by private road.

The view along the rugged Freycinet Peninsula from Sleepy Bay.

Sleepy Bay, Freycinet National Park.

*Fishing boats at St Helens, East Coast. St Helens is
one of the State's most popular holiday resorts.*

The Swansea Bark Mill is the only restored authentic wattle-bark mill in Australia. The original mill, built around 1855 by the Morey family, processed black wattle bark, which was the basic ingredient used for tanning leather.

Morris' General Store in Swansea was built in about 1838 and has been operated by the Morris family for over 100 years. A small museum of items connected with the building is open for inspection during normal trading hours.

Memorial to the Boer War and World Wars I and II, Ross, Midlands. The cannon is a BL 15-powder Mark I used by the Royal Australian Artillery during the Boer War.

Ross Bridge, Midlands. Completed in 1836 at the behest of Lieutenant-Governor George Arthur, the bridge is renowned for its mystical Celtic symbols designed by convict stonemasons Dan Herbert and James Colbeck. The sandstone structure straddles the Macquarie River at the western edge of the historic township of Ross.

The Grange, Campbell Town, was built in 1847 for William Valentine, a doctor, botanist, music-lover and amateur astronomer. In 1874, a number of astronomers from overseas converged upon his observatory to observe the transit of Venus. The Grange was bequeathed to the National Trust in 1964 and is now leased to the Adult Education Board, who use it for hosting residential courses.

The Meander River winds its way gently through the town of Deloraine. This river, which has its origins in the beautiful high country of the Central Plateau, flows eastward from Deloraine to meet the South Esk River near Hadspen.

PREVIOUS PAGE: Liffey Falls. Drawing its water from the Great Western Tiers north of the Great Lake, the Liffey River forms a charming cascade at this popular beauty spot.

N O R T H · W E S T

&

W E S T

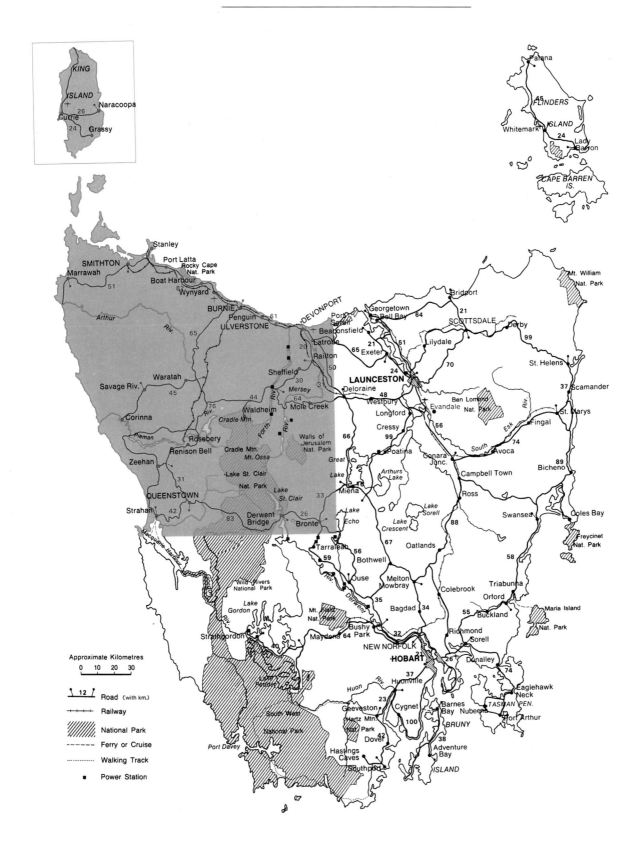

KING
ISLAND
Currie
26 · Naracoopa
24 · Grassy

FLINDERS
ISLAND
45
24
Whitemark
Lady Barron
CAPE BARREN IS.
Patana

Stanley
SMITHTON
Marrawah
51
Port Latta
Rocky Cape Nat. Park
Boat Harbour
83
Wynyard
BURNIE
61
Penguin
ULVERSTONE
65
Arthur Riv.
Savage Riv.
Waratah
45
Corinna
Pieman
76 Riv.
Rosebery
Renison Bell
Zeehan
31
QUEENSTOWN
Strahan
42

DEVONPORT
Port Sorell
Georgetown
Bell Bay
64
Beaconsfield
Latrobe
21
65 Exeter
20
Railton
50
Sheffield
30
Mersey
44 Riv.
64
Waldheim
Mole Creek
Cradle Mtn.
Forth Riv.
Cradle Mtn.
Mt. Ossa
Walls of Jerusalem Nat. Park
Lake St. Clair Nat. Park
Lake St. Clair
33
Derwent Bridge
83
26
Bronte

Bridport
Mt. William Nat. Park
21
SCOTTSDALE
Derby
99
Lilydale
51
70
St. Helens
37 Scamander
LAUNCESTON
24
Deloraine
48
Westbury
Longford
Cressy
99
Poatina
Evandale
Ben Lomond Nat. Park
56
South Esk Riv.
74
Fingal
St. Marys
89 Bicheno
Conara Junc.
Campbell Town
Ross
88
Swansea
Coles Bay
Freycinet Nat. Park
58

66
Great
Lake
Arthurs Lake
Miena
Lake Echo
Lake Sorell
Lake Crescent
67
Oatlands
Tarraleah
56
59
Bothwell
Ouse
Melton Mowbray
35
Bagdad
34
55
Colebrook
Triabunna
Orford
Buckland
Maria Island Nat. Park

Lake Gordon
Strathgordon
Wild Rivers National Park
Lake Pedder
Mt. Field Nat. Park
Maydena
64
Bushy Park
32
NEW NORFOLK
HOBART
26
Dunalley
74
Huon
Riv.
37
Huonville
23
Geeveston
Cygnet
Hartz Mtn. Nat. Park
100
Dover
42
Hastings Caves
Southport
South West National Park
Port Davey
Richmond
Sorell
Eaglehawk Neck
TASMAN PEN.
Port Arthur
Barnes Bay
Nubeena
BRUNY
Adventure Bay
38
ISLAND

Macquarie Harbour

Approximate Kilometres
0 10 20 30

12 Road (with km.)
Railway
National Park
Ferry or Cruise
Walking Track
■ Power Station

For a large number of visitors to Tasmania - those who choose the maritime approach - the first glimpse of the island is of a low shoreline backed by distant hills. As they get closer, buildings appear, and then a town, and a river is entered, shortly after which the Bass Strait ship *Spirit of Tasmania* ties up alongside the quay. This is the city of Devonport, although "city" is somewhat of a misnomer for what is really an enlarged country town of little more than 20,000 people.

Devonport is pleasant enough, but the visitor usually makes tracks fairly quickly, for there is much to explore in the fascinating island that lies beyond. The North-West Coast between Devonport and the industrial town of Burnie is relatively populous by Tasmanian standards, and has suffered much from pollution, but what it lacks in charm and grace is ameliorated by the open friendliness of its people. The growth in population has been dramatic in recent decades: resident numbers in Burnie, Devonport and Ulverstone have all virtually trebled since 1947. The reason is to be found in industrial development and the popularity of the area among retired people (because of its mild climate and good facilities).

West of Burnie are some beautiful patches of coastline, dotted with pleasant little settlements like Boat Harbour and Sisters Beach. Table Cape, near the town of Wynyard, and Rocky Cape, further west, exhibit contrasting beauties which illustrate the region's rich diversity. The former is a bluff which extends into Bass Strait and carries an array of pastoral and arable scenes underlain by a rich soil. It is farming country which cannot fail to please the onlooker. Rocky Cape is original North-West Coast country and is protected as a national park. It is renowned for its wildflowers and Aboriginal relics, and it serves as a valuable ecological refuge, as well as providing a reminder of the vast amount of work done by the region's farmers, past and present, in putting the land to the plough.

In the far North-West, the only towns are Smithton and Stanley. The latter is very old, having once hosted the headquarters of the Van Diemen's Land Company's pastoral empire. It is dominated by a hill known as The Nut which can now be ascended on a chairlift. Inland and west of the administrative centre of Smithton are verdant dairy farms and commercial forests which harbour not only eucalypt but also the native blackwood, an important timber source for Tasmania's furniture-manufacturing industry. On the West Coast, at places like Marrawah and Arthur River, the Southern Ocean rollers pound in ceaselessly. Well to the north, out in Bass Strait, is King Island, another place where waves and wind feature prominently.

The country inland from the Devonport-Burnie area is among the most beautiful in Australia. The juxtaposition of green fields with the wild crags of Mount Roland, the Great Western Tiers and Black Bluff stands comparison with the finest rural scenery anywhere. This is country of peas, poppies and potatoes, cabbages, carrots and cauliflowers. It is also the site of an artificial lake which demonstrates that a dammed river - when treated with sensitivity - may indeed produce a result which is intensely pleasing to the senses. Lake Barrington, near Sheffield, is a beautiful place which has been adopted by lovers of water sports. It is now recognised as possessing one of the world's best rowing courses.

This is also the country of big-boned, broad-shouldered axemen who can lay claim to being among the world's best. For wood-choppers who have grown up on a diet of iron-hard eucalypt, the softwoods of North America fall apart like butter under a hot knife. Many world-champion axemen hail from this part of northern Tasmania, and for the visitor who wishes to see a genuine display of wholesome Tasmaniana there is no better occasion than a wood-chopping carnival.

Further inland still are the wild lands of the central western mountains. Increasingly on the visitor's "must see" list is Cradle Mountain, at the northern end of the Cradle Mountain - Lake St Clair National Park. Renowned for its glacial landforms and dramatic scenery, as well as its abundant wildlife, Cradle Mountain provides the northernmost entry point to Tasmania's World Heritage Area. This is marvellous country for bushwalkers, many of whom traverse the eighty-kilometre Overland Track to Lake St Clair.

The park can also be approached by motor vehicle from Derwent Bridge, at the Lake St Clair end. The Lyell Highway in this area passes through some wild mountain scenery and, in winter, a successful negotiation of the shoulder of Mount Arrowsmith cannot be taken for granted, for the road is often snow-bound. Many first-class short walks are to be found along this important tourist route; one of the most notable is at the junction of the highway with the famous Franklin River.

East of the Cradle Mountain - Lake St Clair National Park is the Central Plateau wilderness, including the Walls of Jerusalem National Park. This is an elevated and exposed region, unique in Australia, where dominant features of the landscape are woodlands and forests of native pencil pine. Heavily glaciated during the Ice Age, the plateau is dotted by thousands of ice-carved lakes and tarns, many of which are stocked with trout.

West of these mountains is the "West Coast" mining region (somewhat misnamed because most of the population centres are well inland). Old settlements like Williamsford and Gormanston are now virtual ghost towns, while others like Queenstown, Rosebery, Waratah, Zeehan and Savage River hang on, hopeful that more mineral fields will be discovered in the vicinity. When this region boomed late last century, it was accessible only by sea, and many of the people felt as closely allied to Melbourne as they did to Hobart (and fairly aloof from both). The West Coasters are a breed apart, and they do not mind telling one so.

Zeehan was once the biggest town in the area, and it developed a reputation for hard work and hard play. As is common in mining centres, it underwent a drastic reduction in population, and it has not been without its modern disasters. A tragic bushfire in 1981 swept part of the town and destroyed forty homes. Queenstown is now the largest centre, but its future is uncertain, as the copper ore at nearby Mount Lyell becomes more costly to extract.

Thankfully, the economic base of the West has diversified somewhat, with tourism, forestry, fishing and fish farming now providing a significant degree of employment. Much more can, and should, be made of the region's tourism potential, for it has a great deal to offer. There is wild scenery, a pioneering spirit, an invigorating climate and relics of the mining industry which are not easily found elsewhere in Tasmania. There are superb river cruises on the Pieman and Gordon Rivers. The latter runs out of the charming port of Strahan on Macquarie Harbour. Most of all, it is an intangible - the spirit of the West - that most strongly appeals to the visitor. Here is a land which, for all its access to the modern world, has kept the effete niceties of life at arm's length. It has a strength which lingers in one's senses.

Limestone formations, Marakoopa Caves, west of Mole Creek. A spreading series of caverns, this subterranean feature - much loved for its glow-worms - is one of many in the limestone-riddled hillsides around Mole Creek. It is open to the general public.

Seen here across picturesque farmland and forest near Deloraine, the Great Western Tiers announce the beginning of the highlands, and beckon the traveller into the state's western wilderness.

A giant Tasmanian devil advertises the entrance to
the Tasmanian Wildlife Park near Mole Creek.

*FAR RIGHT: A familiar symbol of
Australia rests on a tree in the Tasmanian
Wildlife Park. The koala does not occur
in the wild in Tasmania.*

RIGHT: A Tasmanian devil indulges its hearty appetite at the Tasmanian Wildlife Park. The devil is a carnivorous marsupial, now restricted to Tasmania, which has a fearsome reputation thanks to its powerful jaws and often fractious temperament.

BELOW: The ancient Australian musical art of playing the gum leaf is thought to have been learned by humans from native marsupials. A Bennett's wallaby in the Tasmanian Wildlife Park practises for the local championships.

PREVIOUS PAGE: One of Tasmania's most famous landmarks, the dolerite ridge of Cradle Mountain (1,545 metres) rises high above Dove Lake. Some of the finest bushwalking country in Australia is to be found in this vicinity.

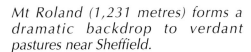

Mt Roland (1,231 metres) forms a dramatic backdrop to verdant pastures near Sheffield.

Bell's Parade and the peaceful Mersey River, Latrobe. One of the oldest towns in the North-West, Latrobe was a busy port before the establishment of berthing facilities at nearby Devonport.

The patchwork of red-brown and green of rich farmland near Forth.

The Mersey River and the compact city of Devonport, seen from the east. The chocolate-coloured soils on the city's outskirts are among the most fertile in the nation.

RIGHT: A place of light and shade. Midday sunshine bathes the Rooke Street Mall in Devonport.

An echo of the days when steam was king. The Van Diemen Light Railway Society's headquarters at Don, just outside Devonport, boast a number of old trains, some of which operate on their own section of the track.

Devonport on the Mersey River, now a city of 25,000 people. For many a visitor who arrives by sea, Devonport is the gateway to Tasmania.

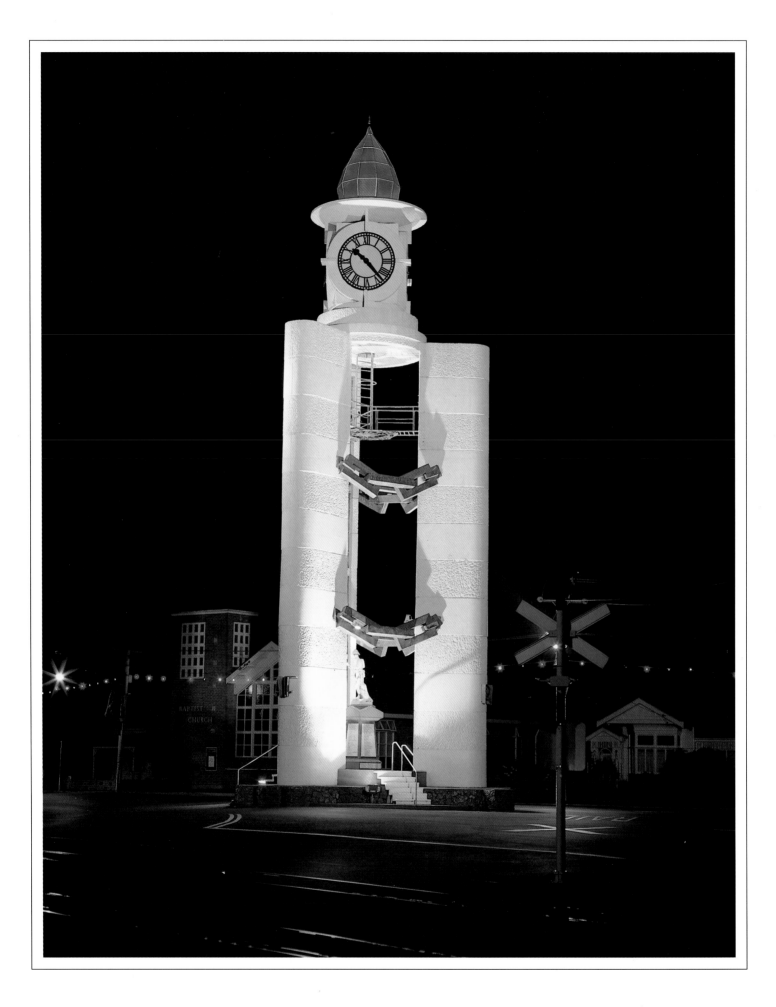

Night adds dramatic effect to Ulverstone's War Memorial Clock Tower. Opened on 1 February 1954, the monument was built on the town's cenotaph, around an existing memorial to the 1914-18 war. The three gigantic columns represent the nation's three armed services.

ABOVE: Spectacular rows of gold, crimson, pink and alabaster greet the visitor to the tulip farm at Wynyard.

LEFT: An unmistakable symbol of an unusually named town. Penguin, on the North-West Coast, was settled by English colonists from the county of Norfolk in about 1860. Its name derives from the numerous fairy-penguin rookeries along this coast.

Inquisitive locals, Table Cape.

The mouth of the Inglis River, Wynyard. Situated 18 kilometres west of Burnie, Wynyard is one of the North-West's most attractive towns.

Farmland abuts on to the healthy ridge of Rocky Cape National Park, between Wynyard and Stanley. This national park is 3,070 hectares of attractive coastline heath and scrub, one of the few parts of the North-West Coast to be preserved in its natural state.

The waters of Bass Strait wash on to Boat Harbour Beach, west of Wynyard.

Stanley is dominated by "The Nut", which rises to 150 metres above the town. This fishing port, endowed with a quiet charm, is one of Tasmania's oldest settlements, having been the site for the headquarters of the Van Diemen's Land Company. It was also the birthplace of one-time Australian Prime Minister Joseph Lyons.

RIGHT: Coastline, Rocky Cape National Park.

Administrative centre of the Circular Head municipality, the town of
Smithton services an area renowned for its productive farms.

RIGHT: An inviting track through wet forest
near Lake Chisholm.

ABOVE: The Hellyer River at Hellyer Gorge on the Murchison Highway south of Yolla. The river is named after Henry Hellyer, a surveyor for the Van Diemen's Land Company between 1826 and 1832, who was one of the region's foremost explorers.

RIGHT: The West Coast Pioneers Memorial Museum in the mining town of Zeehan. Formerly the School of Mines and Metallurgy, the Museum is the town's major tourist drawcard. In its heyday, Zeehan was Tasmania's third-largest population centre.

The Lyell Highway descends into the copper-mining centre of Queenstown.

Snaking through a barren wasteland, the Lyell Highway to Hobart climbs out of Queenstown. The vegetationless "lunar" landscape is the product of over-zealous tree felling and the emission of poisonous smelter fumes in Queenstown's heyday. The native flora, however, is slowly creeping back across these hills.

A view across part of Queenstown to the rugged West Coast Range.

SOUTH-WEST

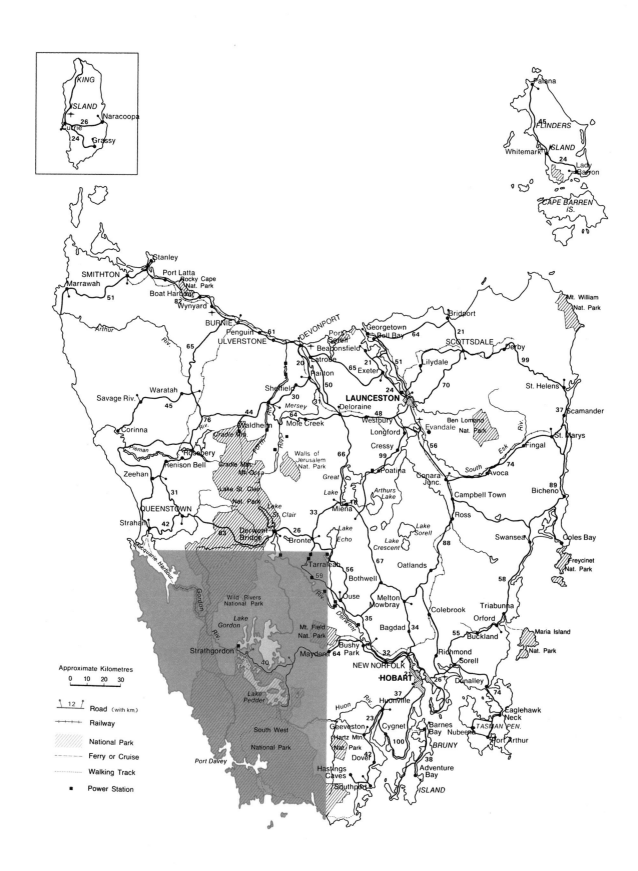

KING
ISLAND
Naracoopa
26
Currie
24
Grassy

Farana
FLINDERS
45
ISLAND
Whitemark
24
Lady
Barron
CAPE BARREN
IS.

Stanley
SMITHTON
Port Latta
Rocky Cape
Nat. Park
Marrawah
Boat Harbour
51
82
Wynyard
BURNIE
Penguin 61
ULVERSTONE
DEVONPORT
Port
Sorell
Georgetown
Bell Bay
64
21
SCOTTSDALE
Derby
Arthur
Riv.
65
Beaconsfield
Latrobe
20
Railton
65 Exeter
51
Lilydale
99
Savage Riv.
Waratah
45
50
Sheffield
24
70
St. Helens
76
44
30
LAUNCESTON
Deloraine
37 Scamander
Corinna
Riv.
Mersey
64
Mole Creek
Westbury
48
Ben Lomond
Nat. Park
St. Marys
Cradle Mtn.
Waldheim
Walls of
Jerusalem
Nat. Park
66
Longford
Cressy
56
Evandale
Rosebery
Mt Ossa
Great
99
Eardley
74
Zeehan
Henison Bell
Lake St. Clair
Nat. Park
Lake
Poatina
Conara
Junc.
Avoca
Bicheno
89
31
Lake
St. Clair
Lake
Campbell Town
QUEENSTOWN
33
Miena
Arthurs
Lake
Ross
Swansea
Coles Bay
Strahan
42
26
Lake
Echo
Lake
Sorell
88
Derwent
Bridge
83
Bronte
Lake
Crescent
Freycinet
Nat. Park
Macquarie Harbour
Tarraleah
56
67
Oatlands
58
Gordon
Riv.
59
Bothwell
Wild Rivers
National Park
Riv.
Ouse
Colebrook
Triabunna
Lake
Gordon
35
Melton
Mowbray
Orford
Mt. Field
Nat. Park
Bagdad
34
55
Buckland
Maria Island
Strathgordon
Bushy
Park
64
Richmond
Sorell
Nat. Park
40
Maydena
NEW NORFOLK
32
Lake
Pedder
HOBART
26
Dunalley
74
Huon
Riv.
Huonville
37
Eaglehawk
Neck
South West
National Park
Huon
Geeveston
23
Cygnet
Barnes
Bay Nubeena
TASMAN PEN.
Port Arthur
Hartz Mtn.
Nat. Park
100
BRUNY
Port Davey
Dover
38
Adventure
Bay
Hastings
Caves
42
Southport
ISLAND

Approximate Kilometres
0 10 20 30

12 Road (with km.)
Railway
National Park
Ferry or Cruise
Walking Track
Power Station

111

In the temperate zones of Earth, there are very few extensive areas of true wilderness left. Even in the non-temperate zones, despite a growing global concern over the fate of the biosphere - upon which humankind must ultimately depend for its survival - the last frontiers are being pushed further and further back, leaving ever smaller patches of pristine ecosystem which, in their turn, are ever more easily defiled as they become accessible to developmental forces. Tasmania, then, has a global significance, for its western regions harbour one of the last great areas of temperate wilderness in the world.

The finest part of this wilderness lies south of the Lyell Highway and west of Maydena, and in all this broad area there are only two major roads - to Strathgordon and Scotts Peak -which, however, penetrate the very heart of the region, nearly cutting it in two. The roads were built in the 1960s for the construction of the enormous Middle Gordon hydroelectric scheme. The Gordon River - Tasmania's mightiest - was dammed, forming the gigantic impoundment of Lake Gordon which is unfortunately characterized by dead trees and muddy shorelines. To the south, the storage was increased by the damming of the Serpentine and Huon Rivers, destroying the original Lake Pedder, one of the world's most beautiful lakes and home to a unique biota. For many of those who knew the lake well, its destruction highlighted the philosophical divide between exploiters and conservers. By a combination of luck and management, however, the new Lake Pedder, which is more accessible to the general public than Lake Gordon, is not unattractive because it swamped an area largely devoid of trees and because it is surrounded by some of Tasmania's most spectacular mountains.

In contrast with much of the world, where roads and motor vehicles are hard to escape, the South-West is primarily the realm of shanks's pony, where the rhythms of nature, rather than the timetables of urban society, order the events of the traveller who seeks solace in that wild land. Neither is the fitness that derives from bushwalking merely physical, for the greatest gift of the wilderness experience (when one is away from roads for several days, or even weeks) is the emotional release that allows the walker to explore his own psyche and which often challenges the roots of his spirituality. The Aborigines - ultimate wilderness dwellers - knew this world like no others ever could. For them, standing rocks, animals, rivers, distant mountains and even the wind itself bore the spirit forces of their ancestors and creators. For many of the early European explorers and pioneers, too, this wild land had a savage magnificence from which the challenge was more than simply physical. It is a well-trodden region but, thanks to the resilience of nature and the minor impact of earlier users, its wilderness quality is, in general terms, of the highest order.

Much of the South-West was regularly burned by the Aborigines - and since their time by later Tasmanians - and, as a result, wide tracts of lowland and highland country bear no forest. On the plains, the vegetation is dominated by the hummock sedge commonly known as "button-grass" and by shrubs of the paperbark and tea-tree genera. On the infertile siliceous mountains, moorland and alpine heath predominate. However, patches of highland rainforest (including the endemic King Billy pine) and lowland rainforest (usually dominated by myrtle, beech and sassafras) do occur in places, and some of these stands are very extensive. Rainforests are undoubtedly special communities, and few people remain unmoved by their rich odours and cool, humid atmospheres. In the South-West, they are garlanded with the endemic climbing heath which, in late summer, stabs the verdant darkness of the forest with a plethora of crimson flowers.

For the romantically inclined, the names in this wild mountainous region peel easily off the tongue and engender immediate enthusiasm in company which has experienced its unique pleasures. Names like Prion Beach, the Ironbound Range, Surprise Bay,

Lake Rhona, Mount Anne, the Lost World Plateau and Bathurst Harbour need only be whispered to the present writer to quicken his pulse and release an involuntary flow of thoroughly wonderful memories.

The Western Arthur Range is perhaps the most spectacular series of mountains in Australia, and in recent years it has become such a popular bushwalking venue that track erosion is now becoming a serious liability. It is easy to see why it is so popular. Along its serrated length are dozens of peaks and precipices, and numerous alpine lakes. However, it is not country for the beginning bushwalker. The wet and windy climate, combined with the range's difficulty of egress (there are only three straightforward routes on and off its entire length) make it a dangerous environment for those of limited experience. The same applies to most of the South-West; those who venture into its wilds must have served an apprenticeship elsewhere, learning to read maps and navigate, and developing an understanding of the equipment and skills necessary for survival should snow and gales arrive or should the rivers become impassable.

The remote nature of the South-West prior to the 1960s is best exemplified by 1,224-metre-high Federation Peak on the eastern extremity of the Eastern Arthur Range, which was first climbed as late as 1949. Earlier attempts had been stymied by bad weather and the region's remoteness. Nowadays, however, the peak can be climbed - by a fast-moving party - in a long weekend.

In addition to the bushwalker, the South-West is also frequented by increasing numbers of people who do not don walking boots. Sailors and aerial day-trippers go into the Port Davey - Bathurst Harbour area, where tin miners still operate their small leases at Melaleuca. Trout fishermen frequent Lake Pedder in large numbers, as do car-based holidaymakers, some of whom find accommodation at Strathgordon. Apiarists seasonally bring in large numbers of beehives to make use of the honey flow from the acclaimed leatherwood tree, a native of the Tasmanian rainforests.

The northern part of the South-West is readily accessible from the Lyell Highway and from the western seaport of Strahan on Macquarie Harbour. In the latter case, the destination is usually the magnificent Gordon River, once the haunt of doughty piners who cut Huon pine from its dense forests. Another attraction of this wild and historic area is Sarah Island in Macquarie Harbour, the site of a dreaded penal settlement in the early nineteenth century, and still bearing some ruins from that period. It is a wild and beautiful place, and it is difficult to imagine the injustice and cruelty which must have afflicted the society that so misused it. There are few better places to ponder the pros and cons of modern Tasmanian society vis-a-vis its earliest post-Aboriginal expression.

Along the Lyell Highway, occasional glimpses may be had of one of Tasmania's most spectacular mountains - Frenchman's Cap. This quartzite peak and its neighbours are partially encircled by the Franklin River, the focus of Australia's greatest conservation conflict in the late 1970s and early 1980s. Preserved from a hydro-electric dam on the Lower Gordon River, this region is now protected in the Franklin - Lower Gordon Wild Rivers National Park, one of the three wilderness national parks which constitute Tasmania's World Heritage Area.

Renowned conservationist Olegas Truchanas once said of Tasmania that it could become a "shining beacon in a dull, uniform and largely artificial world". One can only say how right he was. Ultimately, it is the magnificence of the South-West and Tasmania's other wild places which will provide that inspirational illumination. Much of the West is already on the World Heritage list, and as the region becomes better known to the global community - and to Tasmanians themselves - its prestige will surely grow. Tasmania may yet become the place that Truchanas foresaw - an inspiration for all the world

The Bird River races through rainforest tracts which display a typically lush mixture of species.

The sheer pillars of Mt Anne dominate a foreground of pandanis on the North-East Ridge.